youthwriterscamp.com

---

in partnership with
Youth Enterprise, Inc.

GREETINGS TO ALL!

Welcome to those who have decided to give this young author's first book a read. We believe in youth and their stories so much that we believed we could be a part of helping them to tell them and change them.

Our Youth Writers Camp provides continuous opportunities for healthy emotional expression within a safe and supportive community. Our goal is to not only help young people cope through writing, but also to motivate them to develop their own streams of revenue.

When Thunder Speaks, LLC is actively engaging today's youth with an aim to increase mental and emotional health outcomes. However, we understand that our efforts to positively impact the mental and emotional health of this current generation won't reach maximum effectiveness unless we have the support of the entire community. *THIS IS WHERE YOU COME IN.*

Through the things they discovered about themselves, the lessons about mental health, and the coping techniques they garnered during this time, it is our job as a community to continue to cultivate it and empower them to shift their own realities into the best versions designed for them. Our hope is that these students feel loved, cared for, and equipped enough to continue to heal and process with healthy coping tools and creative avenues. Thank you for investing into this student, one poem at a time.

Brandon Allen, Founder of When Thunder Speaks, LLC

Poets Are Children Too!

Poets Are Children Too!

by Amaryllis Greene

*I dedicate this book to my mom because
I want to thank her for being there for
me along this whole entire journey.*

Contents

Foreword

Dear Amaryllis Greene:

From the day you were conceived our journey together was a test of time. I thought I lost you when I saw the blood stain, yet, in my womb you sustained as Dr. Gabbur bought you into this world a week early.

I knew you had a purpose to fulfill and your journey has just begun, yet, I ask that you Pray as God continues to guide & keep a hedge of protection over your mind for awareness, your body for good health and your soul for everlasting peace.

Your heart is full of love, determination & strength, so Stay Focused in all you do and Remember I'm ALWAYS rooting & Your BIGGEST SUPPORTER FOREVER!!!

So Much Love
My Chocolate Baby
Mommy Allison (Scorpion for Life)
Namaste

Poets Are Children Too!

Mice

Mice suffice without humans advice

Mice might come twice or thrice

Some mice devise plans to survive their dislikes

As they are enticed to fight hard

without the protection of a body guard

To Survive in the human's space only to be chased

as they are never embraced

Can you somehow relate to this type of fate sometimes known as HATE!

T.I.P

(Time Is Prime)

Time is always in its Prime

As it climbs to minutes from seconds

With all that it beckons & sometimes reckons

Time is definitely a life lesson

Yet is also man's confession

As he turns and sees his own reflections

Related to his misdirections

Through his imperfections

Shoe Abuse

Some shoes air on the news

Some people check out their reviews

Others just choose to buy them reused

Some take them on a cruise

Shoes can never disapprove yet are overused

But at night they are definitely removed

Oh how People abuse their shoes

 Our Drug

Technology is good for upgrading our life

But also the most dangerous knife

We use technology for stuff like biology

Technology can also destroy apologies

It can destroy the eyes making you blind

making people redefine you

*Technology is a drug that you
can't unplug from its plug*

*All of humanity depends on the new way
instead of the old way*

*We are all addicted and committed to
this drug called technology*

It's always like you need to take another chug

P.S.D
(Pain-Strain-Demise)

*When you cry after someone pries
it becomes your demise*

*Pain may be the main reason you felt the strain
as the blood drained due to this epidemic that
has slain anyone in its lane*

When you contain the pain you carry the burden

*You feel all alone but maintain
and stay in your zone*

Own your emotions and set yourself free

By cutting down the corrupted tree

Hatred

Hate is a state of emotion people visit

*Some people feel hate when
they intimidate another*

*Almost everyone can relate to
someone who feels hate*

as it's an embedded trait throughout the States

*As some parents impregnate
this unhealthy mental state*

which dictates the fate of innocent neonates

raise your hand if you can relate

to the consumption of the gate of Hate

My Heart

Our hearts are a work of art

X-rays show charts of our heart

Sometimes people need to restart their hearts

My heart doesn't work when we're apart

Without you my heart will stop needing to be started again

You're a part of me as I'm a part of you

I thank fate for leading you to me my mate

B.Y.B.Y

(Be Your Best You)

Be Your Best You!

Cause no one else can be you!

Genetically unique from your Head to Your feet.

Not to be compared yet cheered on

As you are designed to Glow & Shine!

Have No Regrets when you take your First Steps

For it's your storyline which co-signs
the time you experienced here

All in All when you got the call,
you gave it your all

Sometimes you may fall so get up Neanderthal

Cause in this life we all encounter curve balls

So keep going

Give it your all

To Be Your Best You!

Feeling Alone
(Part 1)

There are different levels to feeling alone

You all have possibly felt you
were riding a cyclone

It doesn't matter your Skin Tone, what you own,
or expensive cologne

You will always feel alone in different zones;

But there is a good thing about being alone

You find true friends that you can depend on

The Levels
(Part 2)

Level 1 - is to extend and ascend

Level 2 - is when you comprehend

&

Level 3 - is to overextend

These 3 levels can each destroy a person.

Level 1 can destroy the weak-minded

Level 2 can change someone's views

&

*Level 3 can worsen someone to the point
they lose their sanity*

Rapists

He sticks, He clicks, Some Girls my age on the
street trick, what is this happening before my
innocent eyes? Oh how I despise their purity was
lost not by choice, yet, by some who took their
voice!!!!

Who will be there to help them, in their despair?
Their bodies were so young as we were
understood to grow and have Fun.

I believe some are hurt by their horrible
nightmares, as the world didn't fight fair and
denied them their rightful time of being a child

About the Author

Amaryllis Greene is 11 years old and lives in New York. She enjoys reading, writing, acting, and modeling. She absolutely loves meeting new people and completely loves herself.

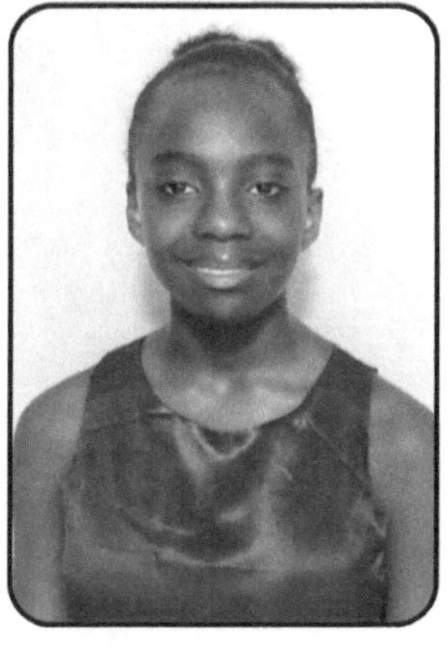

www.ingramcontent.com/pod-product-compliance
Lightning Source LLC
Chambersburg PA
CBHW020836150726
48196CB00002B/85